The Season of Hope

A companion

through

the Days of

Advent & Christmas

Cathie Talbot

The Season of Hope
A companion through the Days of Advent & Christmas

WoodLake

Editor: Michael Schwartzentruber
Cover design: Verena Velten
Cover artwork: *Stars and Seven Sheep*, copyright © John Borden Evans.
    Used by permission.
Interior design: Margaret Kyle and Julie Bachewich
Proofreader: Dianne Greenslade

WoodLake is an imprint of Wood Lake Books, Inc. Wood Lake Books acknowledges the financial support of the Government of Canada, through the Book Publishing Industry Development Program (BPIDP) for its publishing activities.

At Wood Lake Books, we practice what we publish, being guided by a concern for fairness, justice, and equal opportunity in all of our relationships with employees and customers. Wood Lake Books is an employee-owned company, committed to caring for the environment and all creation. Wood Lake Books recycles, reuses, and encourages readers to do the same. Resources are printed on 100% post consumer recycled paper and more environmentally friendly groundwood papers (newsprint), whenever possible. A percentage of all profit is donated to charitable organizations.

Library and Archives Canada Cataloguing in Publication
Talbot, Cathie, 1952–
The season of hope: a companion through the days of Advent & Christmas/Cathie Talbot.
ISBN 1-55145-520-X
    1. Advent – Prayer-books and devotions – English. 2. Christmas – Prayer-books and
    devotions – English. I. Title.
BV40.T34 2006   242'.33   C2006-900928-7

Published by WoodLake, an imprint of Wood Lake Publishing Inc.
9590 Jim Bailey Road, Kelowna, BC, Canada, V4V 1R2
www.woodlakebooks.com
250.766.2778

Printing 10 9 8 7 6 5 4 3 2 1
Printed in Canada by
Houghton Boston Printers, Saskatoon, SK

Acknowledgments

I would like to thank the international and ecumenical community of writers, editors, and resource people who help to create the resources for *Seasons of the Spirit,* a comprehensive and lectionary-based Christian education curriculum for all ages. I am always grateful for the wisdom and insight gained from working collaboratively with such a fine group of people.

In particular, I want to acknowledge John Indermark, writer of the *Seasons of the Spirit Adult* resources, and Jeffrey Nelson, writer of the *Seasons of the Spirit Ages 15–18* resources, for Advent and Christmas 2006–07, who have both provided inspiration for some of the material in this book.

Cathie Talbot

Permissions

Excerpt from *Psalm 25* from *Psalms for Praying: An Invitation to Wholeness* by Nan C. Merrill. Copyright © 1996 by Nan C. Merrill. Reprinted by permission of The Continuum International Publishing Group.

"Hush" by Lucinda Hynett, copyright © Lucinda Hynett. Originally published in *Alive Now.* Used by permission.

"Praying through the Thick of It" by Fredrick Zydek copyright © Fredrick Zydek, as it appeared in *Alive Now,* November/December 2004. Reprinted by permission.

∼ December 1 ∼

God's Promise of Hope

Scripture reading: Jeremiah 33:14–16

The days are surely coming, says God,
when I will fulfill the promise I made…
Jeremiah 33:14a

What does the future hold? We don't know, but the scripture readings for the beginning of Advent invite us to trust God in the midst of uncertain times. In situations that seem only threatening, we hear words that promise restoration. The hope of Advent affirms that a time is coming when God's reign will arrive in our midst, and that we can live in hope rather than in despair.

"The days are surely coming…when I will fulfill the promise I made…" The situation behind these words from the prophet Jeremiah was about as awful as it could be. The Babylonian armies were poised for invasion and Jerusalem and Judah were on the brink of ruin. Yet, surprisingly, Jeremiah offers words of hope in the face of mounting despair and uncertainty. The hope that the prophet speaks of is grounded in the promises of God, with whom nothing is impossible.

Like the people of Judah and Jerusalem, we also live in times of despair and uncertainty. Too often we feel helpless in the face of situations – both personal and global – that are so vast they seem overwhelming. Jeremiah's words remind us that God is a God of promise, and that hope can grow in the midst of anxiety and despair.

Advent means "coming," of course, and the promise of Advent is that what is coming is an unimaginable invasion. The mythology of our age has to do with flying saucers and invasions of outer space, and this is unimaginable enough. But what is upon us now is even more so – a close encounter not of the third kind but of a different kind altogether.

An invasion of holiness. That is what Advent is about.
Frederick Buechner, *Listening to Your Life*

Take a few moments to name some of the anxieties and uncertainties that are part of your life right now. These could be personal, or they might be feelings that come after listening to the morning news. Then imagine that the "days are coming" when you, and those you love, and perhaps the whole planet, will truly experience an "invasion of holiness." Carry this phrase with you as you move through this season of Advent looking for places and moments where God's holiness is invading your life.

Questions for reflection

- In the midst of anxieties and uncertainties, what surprising words of hope do you hear?
- What rituals or activities could you introduce during this Advent to open your heart and mind to an "invasion of holiness"?

Prayer

O God, open my eyes and my soul to see signs of your holiness invading my life. Be with me as I watch and wait. Fill me with the courage of your hope. Amen.

∽ December 2 ∽

Signs of the Times

Scripture reading: Luke 21:25–36

There will be signs in the sun, the moon, and the stars,
and on the earth distress among nations
confused by the roaring of the sea and the waves…
when you see these things taking place,
you know that the dominion of God is near.

Luke 21:25, 31

This reading from the gospel of Luke frames hope in cosmic terms. Jesus lived at a time when apocalyptic thinking – concern about the end times – was prevalent; the ideas conveyed by these words would have been familiar to most people. Jesus points to signs in creation that form an unsettling backdrop of distress and confusion.

Though 2000 years have passed, not much has changed. The images in this passage speak to our own time. *"There will be signs in sun and moon and stars…"* There are those today who would make outer space the next battleground with "star wars" scenarios. Space has become a moral and spiritual arena, full of signs for those who are watching. *"And on earth distress among nations…"* We see evidence of global unrest every time we open a newspaper or turn on the television. Political systems are shifting and poverty is a growing reality for too many people in the world. *"Confused by the roaring of the sea and the waves…"* Warnings about global warming and images of subsequent environmental catastrophes dominate our media and memories. The seas and lakes and oceans of the world sustain our very lives, yet "roaring waves" have also caused destruction and terror.

Semiotics is the study of signs and symbols, including the "signs of the times." What do these signs mean? Do they signal, as some would have us believe, the end of the world as we know it? Or should we see them as a warning, as a reminder of the role we have played in creating these global threats? Where can we find hope in the midst of these times?

"When you see these things taking place, you know that the dominion of God is near…" Jesus offers a surprisingly positive message of hope. He encourages us to trust that, in spite of everything that points to the contrary, God is near. The hopeful waiting that is part of our Advent journey affirms that in the midst of all the distress and confusion, we can still trust in God, who is forming the next chapter of human history.

Questions for reflection

◆ What "signs of the times" speak most clearly to you these days? Some read the "signs of the times" as an ending, a wiping out of the world. Others see these signs as a prelude to new beginnings, the "new thing that God is doing."

◆ What makes it possible for you to live in hopeful anticipation? What helps you trust that God is near?

Prayer

Creator God, help me to live with trust and anticipation. Help me to not succumb to despair and hopelessness but to see the possible behind the pain, and the hope behind the despair. Amen.

Living in Anticipation

Scripture reading: Luke 21:25–36

*Be alert at all times, praying that you may have the strength
to escape all these things that will take place,
and to stand before the Human One.*

Luke 21:36

I
n the reading from the gospel of Luke, Jesus names some "signs
of the times" and then goes on to give some advice: *"Be alert at all
times…"* And what does Jesus say to pray for? *"…the strength to escape
these things that will take place…"*

The future can often make us fearful and fill us with worry.
Universal anxiety seems to be the common trait of our times. Ask any
pastor or priest, doctor, social worker, pharmacist, or counselor, and
they will tell you that life for many people today is full of a constant
and usually unfocused anxiety. Our minds can imagine any number of
"things that will take place," from environmental disaster, to economic
collapse, unemployment, illness, and war. Issues of safety and security
are part of all of these concerns. We wonder what the future holds
for the world's children, perhaps for our own grandchildren. Will the
world we pass on to the next generation hold more or less hope than
the one that we inherited, especially in terms of the environment and
economy?

Sometimes, our anxieties threaten to overwhelm us. We are
tempted to let our *faith* turn into *fate*: "What will be, will be, and

there's nothing we can do about it." But there *are* signs of God's activity among us, even if we don't always see or recognize them. Our faith calls us to a different way of knowing and of being in the world. We know, deep down, that whatever the future may hold, God will be a part of it. Therefore we are called to live not with foreboding, but with anticipation, with hope, until that time when we "stand before the Human One."

Questions for reflection

- In what ways do you find the future promising, threatening, surprising?
- To what extent are your thoughts about the future shaped by present and past experiences?
- How does trusting that God is active in your life affect how you live into the future?

Advent has been called a time of waiting or living with expectation.

- What does it mean to wait with anticipation? What gives you a sense of hope about the future?
- Do you see hope as saving what is slipping away, or as an openness to a surprising and unexpected new thing?

During Advent we think about both the "now" and the "not yet" of God's reign.

- What surprises do you think God might have in store for us in the future?

Prayer

Loving and faithful God, help me to trust the way into your future. Let these coming days transform my practice of discipleship. May I find in you a hope that sustains, a vision that renews, and the Spirit who empowers. Amen.

～ December 4 ～

Trusting in God

Scripture reading: Psalm 25:1–10

To you, O God, I lift up my soul. O my God, in you I trust...
Make me to know your ways, O God; teach me your paths.
Lead me in your truth, and teach me,
for you are the God of my salvation; for you I wait all day long.

Psalm 25:1, 4–6

Psalm 25 is a song of trust, reflecting in personal terms the trust spoken of in the previous readings. When we read these words, it is like being in a conversation with God, pleading for God to teach, lead, and remember. In return, we promise to wait and trust, and to be faithful. The song begins with a statement of trust: *"O my God, in you I trust..."* With each plea and request of God, one can sense the writer's trust in God's steadfast love. How often have you expressed a longing to understand the ways of God? *"Make me to know your ways..."* We know that we can't always understand the ways of God, but we know that we can trust God to be there, no matter what happens.

What does it mean to you to engage in the practice of trust? In today's society, it's easy to become distrustful. We warn our children of "stranger danger." When we are offered something, we wonder what the catch is, what will we have to give or do in return? Yet trust is such a strong theme in the scripture readings for Advent. Perhaps if we can respond to the invitation to trust God, we can begin to live in hope, between the reality of the "now" and the vision of the "not yet."

Questions for reflection

The psalm speaks of trusting God's promises.

♦   What are the words of promise for you in the reading from
    Psalm 25?
♦   When have you had to place your trust in God?
♦   Where might you find help when it feels like a struggle to trust
    in God?

Prayer

Take some time today to "lift up your soul" to God. You might quiet
yourself by using a breath prayer, saying the words (silently or aloud)
"lead me" and "teach me" as you breathe in, and the words "remember
me" as you breathe out. Then read this paraphrase of the psalm as a
prayer.

To You, O Love, I lift up my soul;
O Heart within my heart,
in You I place my trust.
Let me not feel unworthy;
let not fear rule over me.
Yes! Let all who open their hearts
savour You and bless the earth.

Compel me to know your ways, O Love;
instruct me upon your paths.
Lead me in your truth, and teach me,
for through You will I know wholeness.
I shall reflect your light both day and night.

I know of your mercy, Compassionate One,
and of your steadfast love.
You have been with me from the beginning.
Forgive the many times I have
walked away from You
choosing to walk alone.
With your steadfast love, once again,
Companion me along your way.
You are gracious and just,
O Spirit of Truth,
happy to guide those who
miss their way.

You enjoy teaching all who are open,
all who choose to live in truth.
Your paths are loving and sure,
O Holy One,
for those who give witness to You
through their lives.

Nan Merrill, *Psalms for Praying*

∼ December 5 ∼

Lift Up Your Soul

Scripture reading: Psalm 25:1–10

All the paths of God are steadfast love and faithfulness,
for those who keep God's covenant and decrees.

Psalm 25:10

The first ten verses of Psalm 25 contain words of penitence and confession: "you are the God of my salvation…," "don't remember the sins of my youth." They also express a longing for God to "be mindful" and full of mercy. Traditionally, Advent was a penitential season, not unlike Lent. The focus of the season was judgment and repentance. Even the color of the season, purple, was shared with Lent.

In recent times, the focus of Advent has changed from penitence to expectation and hope in the promises of God fulfilled, as Christians believe, in the birth of Jesus. In many churches, the seasonal color for Advent has changed from purple to a deep blue, to symbolize hope and expectation.

Look again at the words of Psalm 25 and see how they function like a bridge between these two understandings of Advent. First, they show an awareness of times when we have walked away from God, choosing to go our own way. Then they express a longing for God to be merciful and to not remember these "transgressions." This attitude of penitence leads us to remember the promise of God's steadfast love and faithfulness. As we trust in this promise, we move from penitence to hope and expectation.

When we "lift up our souls" in prayer, asking God to be mindful of us and becoming aware of the things we want to let go of, we are praying with our lives. We are not searching for God, but rather letting go and waiting in hope and trust. This Advent waiting is not idle, empty time; it is a time of opening ourselves in anticipation of the One who comes, again and again and again. How might you be more mindful during the coming weeks? Where might you carve out some time to "lift up your soul" in prayer and to open your soul and heart in trust?

Questions for reflection

◆ Do you think there is a place for repentance and confession at beginning of Advent? Why or why not?

There is a sense, in the reading from Psalm 25, of being able and willing to change. The psalmist speaks of being open to being taught and led.

◆ In what ways does an attitude of penitence help you to be open and trust in God's promises?

◆ How do you give expression to your trust in God for the future – in the choices you make, in the votes you cast, in the day-to-day decisions that you make, in the witness you offer?

Prayer

O God, to you I lift up my soul. To you I open my heart, trusting in you and acknowledging my need for your steadfast love and faithfulness, especially in the busyness of this month. Amen.

∼ December 6 ∼

Abounding in Love

Scripture reading: 1 Thessalonians 3:9–13

…abound in love for one another and for all…
in order to strengthen your hearts in holiness…

1 Thessalonians 3:12b, 13a

We abound in love for you." Paul seems to have had an amazing gift for affirming people. In his first letter to the Christians in Thessalonica, Paul tells them what a privilege and joy it is for him to know them and how much he looks forward to seeing them again one day. In setting guidelines for a "practice of love" Paul encourages them to *"abound in love for one another and for all."* We, too, can carry these words with us during Advent. The hope that sustains us in these days thrives on the practice of being thankful and on our ability to let love thrive in our lives.

In some traditions, today is the feast day of St. Nicholas, whose legend of giving secret gifts to the poor became the model for the Christian practice of gift giving. We are also called to a practice of love that crosses boundaries, to offer care and acceptance "to all" as well as to "one another." At this time of year, advertising agencies are only too eager to tell us what we must buy and do in order to share that special Christmas joy with everyone we love. We can become frantic trying to consider all those we need to remember to add to our shopping lists.

Paul's words remind us of the real reason we should reach beyond ourselves in love. It is not to add one more gift under the tree, but to practice the kind of love that can *"strengthen our hearts in holiness."* Holiness is something that lives and thrives in the relationships we have with each other and with those beyond the immediate circles of our lives.

The Season of Advent invites us to see how hope and holiness can take shape in the way we care for and love one another, and are cared for and loved by others. Read verse 9 again and think of the one person who best fits this description in your life. Who fills you with joy? Say a prayer of thanks for the presence of this person in your life. Consider giving this person a card or note of thanks. Now spend a few moments thinking of all of those you care for and care about. Reflect on the ways in which you "abound" or are filled with love for each one of these. Then, in the spirit of St. Nicholas, think about the ways in which you can be filled with love for those beyond your immediate circle of family and friends.

Questions for reflection

♦ In what ways are you practicing love that sustains and strengthens your heart in holiness?

Recall the words from Frederick Buechner, who said that Advent was about *"an invasion of holiness."*

♦ In what ways might the practice of love open your heart and mind to an "invasion of holiness"?

Prayer

O God, you are my source of hope and love. Strengthen my heart. Help me to let love thrive in my life throughout this Advent and beyond. Amen.

~ **December 7** ~

Justice and Righteousness

Scripture reading: Jeremiah 33:14–16

…I will cause a righteous Branch to spring up…
and he shall execute justice and righteousness in the land…
Jeremiah 33:15

During Advent, we affirm that we live in hope between the "now" and "not yet" of God's reign. In the readings so far, we have heard words that challenge us to live faithfully toward the future, even as situations, people, and events may try our patience and trust in the present.

Like people in ancient times, we seem to need constant reminders that, frustrating and overwhelming as the present may sometimes be, God is present in this "now."

We sometimes fall into the trap of thinking that God may have been present with people in the past but that current events are so awful that they must have gotten away from God's control. Jeremiah's words remind us that this just isn't so, that God has promised a time when justice and righteousness will prevail. This biblical vision isn't about the coming of comfortable things, but about the kind of security that will come when society provides all living things with justice and safety.

Jeremiah's prophecy about a "righteous branch" springing from the family tree is about one who will come to carry out justice and righteousness, as a sign that God is still active among us. As Christians, we recognize God's reign of justice and righteousness in the coming of

Christ. Our discipleship emerges from the way our trust in that reign takes shape in our living each day. Our Advent hope calls us to write with our lives a new way of living that emphasizes justice and peace.

Questions for reflection

◆ Where are you longing for justice, righteousness, and safety in your own life, and in the lives of others?

◆ Who in our world today is waiting for the execution of God's justice and righteousness?

During Advent, we are called to live in hopeful anticipation.

◆ In what ways does hope help shape the way you live in the "now and not yet" of God's reign?

Prayer

O God, may I never fail to be surprised by your presence and love in my life. Help me to experience a fresh openness to your promises. Help me to be faithful to your vision of peace and justice, and to live with hope. Amen.

∼ December 8 ∼

And You, Child...

Scripture reading: Luke 1:68–79

And you, child, will be called the prophet of the Most High;
for you will go before the Lord, to prepare the ways of the Lord...
Luke 1:76

Often, people refer to the birth of a child as a "blessed event." And so it is. The blessing, though, does not end with the birth. Children can be a blessing *throughout* our lives.

Children can also be *recipients* of our blessings, as we hear in this reading from the first chapter of the gospel of Luke. In these verses, we hear a parent's song to a newborn child; we hear words of both celebration and promise, the joy brought by a long-awaited child and the awareness that this child will be someone very special.

Both Zechariah and Elizabeth were descendants of Aaron, the first high priest of the Jewish faith. The gospel story tells us that Zechariah was serving in the temple when he experienced a vision, an angel announcing the news that his wife Elizabeth, though elderly like himself, would bear a child. Understandably, Zechariah finds this news almost impossible to believe and is struck speechless.

After the child is born, Zechariah, filled with the Holy Spirit, speaks a blessing over his son, John, and identifies his future role: *"And you, child, will be called the prophet of the Most High..."* With these words, Zechariah trusts and entrusts the blessing and promises of God upon John, who will become John the Baptizer. Zechariah blesses his newborn child and that blessing cascades into promises of hope for the people. Think about the children in your own life and reflect on how they have given blessing to you.

Zechariah's song of blessing is a song about life, self, and God. Imagine being present at the birth of a baby. Imagine that you are the first person this child sees and hears as she or he comes into the world. What would you like to tell this child about him- or herself, beginning with the words, "And you child, will be…" What would you like to tell this child about the world? What would you like to tell this child about God?

Questions for reflection

◆ What do you hear in Zechariah's blessing that affirms your life, your call?

Imagine that similar words were spoken to you at your birth: "And you, child, will be called…"

◆ How do you think those who loved and cared for you would complete this sentence?

◆ What might it feel like to speak such a blessing over your own child?

Think about the children and youth you know.

◆ How do they help you to live with hope in the "now" and the "not yet" of God's reign?

Prayer

God of wonder and delight, open me to the blessing that has been mine since birth. Help me to know that blessing in the core of my being, and to share the gift of that blessing with the children in my life. Amen.

~ December 9 ~

Prepare the Way

Scripture reading: Malachi 3:1–4

See, I am sending my messenger to prepare the way before me…
Malachi 3:1a

Many of the scripture readings for Advent speak of a messenger and a message. These verses from the prophet Malachi announce a messenger who is coming to prepare the way. Furthermore, they warn that God's messenger and God's message can break into human affairs without warning.

Messengers come to interpret the signs of the times for us. They prepare us for something that is coming. The prophet Malachi uses some strong words to describe the actions of God's messenger: he will come *suddenly; refining, cleansing, and purifying.* This is how God prepares us and God's ways are not always comfortable.

Reflect on the images that come to mind as you think about the phrase "like a refiner's fire," from Malachi 3:2. The word "refine" means "to remove impurities" in order to produce a purer form of something, or "to make something more effective" by improving it through small changes. In what ways do you think that your life needs "refining"? What are some of the impurities that need to be removed? What small changes might you consider in order to make your living more effective?

Malachi also speaks of the messenger being like "fuller's soap." A "fuller," in biblical times, was one who fulls or thickens, cleanses, bleaches, and sometimes dyes cloth in the process of making it or caring for it. The fullers used lye or a special kind of soap to loosen the grime in cloth before it was washed.

There are messages and messengers in every time. In a way, each of us is called to be a messenger, to prepare the way for the coming of God's reign. Sometimes what we do and what we say can open the way to an experience of God's presence. Reflect on the phrase "like fuller's soap." In what ways can your actions and words during Advent be like "fuller's soap," loosening the "grime" of injustice and apathy that pervade our world?

Questions for reflection

♦ What are you doing to prepare your life for what God is working out?
♦ What are the most important things this reading says to you about yourself and about God?

The reading from Malachi makes it clear that the way God breaks into our lives may not be all that comfortable sometimes.

♦ In what ways has God's presence been like a refining, purifying fire for you? For the world?

Prayer

God of the prophets, you call me to announce your reign of justice, peace, and truth in a world that desperately needs these things. Open me to be refined, washed, and purified, so that I, too, can be your messenger of hope. Amen.

The Voice of One Crying

Scripture reading: Luke 3:1–6

John went into all the region around the Jordan,
proclaiming a baptism of repentance for the forgiveness of sins…
Luke 3:3

Christian tradition identifies John the Baptizer as the messenger spoken of in Malachi's prophecy. The child who received a blessing and commissioning from his father, Zechariah, does become a "prophet of the Most High." John announces the promise of God's reign and sees his role as the one to prepare the way for Jesus, God's Messiah.

Yet John seems to be an unlikely choice for a prophet. When we look at the first few verses of the third chapter of Luke's gospel, we see a careful listing of "very important persons" in their "very important places." From these important rulers in high places the people might expect big things. But the surprise is that the announcement of the new thing God is doing doesn't come from these VIPs in centers of power, but from somewhere and someone totally unexpected. Instead, a messenger comes from the wilderness, bearing a vision of change. And he brings a message that seems to be more warning than blessing. John proclaims a *"baptism of repentance,"* announcing that everything must turn around in order for the new vision to dawn.

John's work of announcing and preparing remains to be done, even today. We have a long way to go before we'll see a world where all walk in the way of peace. We live between the times, aware of the realities in our own lives and in the world around us, and for which we need to ask forgiveness.

As you move through the days of Advent, consider those ways of living, of thinking, of acting that need to be "turned around" in your life, so that you will be ready to welcome the child in the manger.

Questions for reflection

♦ What turning and repenting do you need to do in your life?
♦ Who are the voices calling you to turn around in your lifestyle, in your attitudes?

Living prophetically means, in part, living with a hope that reaches beyond the reality of the world.

♦ How are you living prophetically in your daily life?

Prayer

Almighty God, whose wisdom and insight exceeds all understanding, give me courage to acknowledge the places where I need to "turn around," where I need to ask for forgiveness. Amen.

~ December 11 ~

Prepare the Way

Scripture reading: Luke 3:1–6

Every valley shall be filled, and every mountain and hill made low,
and the crooked shall be made straight,
and the rough ways made smooth…

Luke 3:5

The word of God came to John, son of Zechariah, in the wilderness…" The gospel of Luke doesn't give us a description of John, this prophet from the wilderness. The gospel of Mark tells us that he was "clothed in camel hair, with a leather belt around his waist" and that his diet included "locusts and wild honey." John is depicted as someone who spent time in the wilderness and who perhaps saw life from a different perspective than his contemporaries. Think about this description of John. Who exemplifies this kind of messenger, or prophet, in our world today?

Being a prophet can mean facing the realities of the world with a different and sometimes unpopular viewpoint. The reading from the first part of chapter three in Luke's gospel tells us that the way God breaks open, the way that is being prepared, may not be all that comfortable to travel. It speaks about crooked ways needing to be made straight and rough ways needing to be smoothed out.

It is easy to imagine the damage boulders and bumps on a highway can do to a car and the people in it. We want and need a clear way for our physical journeys. And we need to clear the way for our spiritual journey also. During Advent, we are called to remove the obstacles, the boulders and bumps, that block the work of God's Spirit. Preparing for God means removing, as much as we can, things like selfishness and bickering and laziness.

It can also mean considering the protective walls and security screens that we have erected around ourselves. To meet others, we sometimes have to prepare the way by taking down the barriers we have built between ourselves and others. We need to let go of everything that tries to oppress or possess or alienate, in order to make the rough places smooth.

Questions for reflection

The "word of God" that came to John is a message of salvation for all: "Clear the way for God is coming."

◆ Who are the voices crying from the wilderness today, urging us to prepare the way for God?

◆ What do you need to let go of, or remove, or smooth out, in order to open the way for the work of God's Spirit?

Prayer

Creator God, help me to prepare for your coming by removing attitudes that oppress or alienate. Help me to be aware of and let go of the things that block the work of your Spirit. Amen.

~ **December 12** ~

Holding in the Heart

Scripture reading: Philippians 1:3–11

…you hold me in your heart,
for all of you share in God's grace with me…
Philippians 1:7b

P aul begins his letter to the Philippians by thanking God for the times he spent with them in Philippi. He goes on to say that he is "constantly praying with joy" for all of the believers there.

There are many people we "hold in our hearts," particularly at this time of year. What difference might it make in your life, and in the lives of those you pray for, if you were to "constantly pray with joy" for those people whom you hold dear? Some people seem to have a special ability to live their days in an attitude of prayer. Advent is a time when we are encouraged to be more intentional about practicing spiritual disciplines. In the midst of the busyness, consider the ways in which you might take time to pray for those you hold in your heart, remembering them as you write your Christmas cards, as you do your gift shopping, as you make time for phone calls, as you worship.

Paul also affirms the community of Christians in Philippi. It is amazing how frequently we forget or neglect to affirm others in our community. We take it for granted that family members, friends, fellow members of our church, even the pleasant cashier at the grocery story, all know that they are appreciated. We assume that people will know without being told that their contributions are valued and that we enjoy their company. Yet we all know what it feels like to be taken for granted. We all have a need to be in relationships where our deepest selves are affirmed in tangible ways.

As Caryll Houselander prays, "O God who comes to us in the thousands of faces we meet this Advent, help us to recognize ourselves in them, to welcome them, and so to welcome you."

Consider how you might live the days during Advent in more prayerful, affirming ways.

Questions for reflection

♦ Who do you "hold in your heart"? When was the last time you offered them words of affirmation?

♦ In what ways might you affirm and give thanks for those who you meet?

Prayer

Loving God, I give thanks for the many people who have enriched my life. I pray that I might let your love and care flow through me, so that all may know and experience your amazing grace. Amen.

～ December 13 ～

Overflowing Love

Scripture reading: Philippians 1:3–11

*And this is my prayer, that your love may overflow
more and more with knowledge and full insight.*
Philippians 1:9

I n his letter to the Philippians, Paul expresses a longing that the believers in Philippi will know how much they are loved by God and by others in the community. Notice the kind of love that Paul speaks about in this chapter – one that is "full of knowledge and insight" (some translations say "full of knowledge and discernment"). The love that Paul is speaking about is not the kind of sentimental love conjured up by so many ad campaigns at this time of year. It is a love that is grounded in reality; a love that continues because of, and sometimes in spite of, what we come to know about ourselves and about each other.

We were created by love, for love, and so that we should love. "Before I formed you in the womb, I knew you," is what God said to Jeremiah. These are words that apply to each of us. We were planned for from all eternity. None of us is a mere divine afterthought. None of us is an accident… There is nothing you can do that will make God love you less. There is nothing you can do to make God love you more. God's love for you is infinite, perfect, and eternal.
Archbishop Desmond Tutu, An African Prayer Book

Paul goes on to say that it is his prayer that *"love will overflow more and more with knowledge and full insight..."* Focus on verses nine and ten. Imagine that Paul is praying this prayer for you. Imagine the love that you have for yourself, for God, and for others, overflowing with knowledge and insight. There is a line in a prayer that says, "To view the world through love-filled eyes, be patient, understanding, gentle, wise." In what ways are you able to view the world through love-filled eyes?

Paul also encourages his readers to use a loving way of life to create a "harvest of righteousness." Another way to describe righteousness is to call it "right living," but then it is easy to think that being righteous has something to do with being "right." The Hebrew word for righteous comes from the word *tzadeek,* which means "just" or "fair." A righteous one is a person who sees the injustice in the world and tries to bring more justice to it. Consider how the knowledge that you are loved can encourage you to work for peace and justice, part of the "harvest of righteousness."

Questions for reflection

♦ What does it mean to you to know that you are "created by love, for love, in order to love"?

♦ In what ways have you experienced overflowing love in your life?

♦ How might your love overflow during this season, enabling you to work for the peace and justice that the world longs for?

Prayer

Fill me, O God, with your loving presence. Let my life overflow with your love. Help me to view the world through love-filled eyes, to live justly and fairly. Amen.

∼ December 14 ∼

Into the Way of Peace

Scripture reading: Luke 1:68–79

...the dawn from on high will break upon us,
to give light to those who sit in the night and in the shadow of death,
to guide our feet into the way of peace.

Luke 1:79

I n this reading from the gospel of Luke, Zechariah is aged, near the end of his life. John is an infant, with his whole life before him. For most parents, the birth of a child encourages them to reflect on their own lives, and on what the future may hold for their child.

In his prophetic song of blessing, Zechariah focuses on the hope that John will bring an awareness of God's action in the midst of the people, and a whole new awareness of the way in which life should be lived. Zechariah's song begins by announcing the coming of a "mighty saviour," who will remember and restore and rescue and show mercy. It goes on to say that John will be a prophet, who will prepare the way for this saviour, and who will call the people to live with justice and righteousness. Finally, the song ends with a promise of peace.

Two of the most beautiful parts of Zechariah's blessing are the phrases *"to give light to those who sit in the night"* and *"to guide our feet into the way of peace."* Amidst the political domination and religious division of Luke's day, Zechariah's blessing affirmed that God would deliver the people from the oppression of Roman rule. In our world today, people still experience political domination and religious division. We still need this promise that God will give light to those who sit in night, and that God will guide us in the ways of mercy and peace.

Focus on the words in Luke 1:78–79 again. Think about the "new dawn" you are waiting for in your own life. Then think about the "new dawn" people are longing for in so many places around the world. Consider the ways that you might help to make this Advent and Christmas season a "new dawn" for yourself and for others.

Questions for reflection

Think about the places and situations where people today are looking for peace and for ways in which they can live without fear.

♦ Who speaks words of hope and advocates for justice and peace in circumstances?

Zechariah called his son a prophet.

♦ Have you ever thought of yourself as a prophet? Why or why not?

♦ In what ways might you be a prophet, preparing the way for God's peace and justice?

Prayer

Faithful God, I ask for courage and insight to live prophetically in all the places of my life. Guide my feet into the way of peace, now and always. Amen.

⌒ December 15 ⌒

What Should We Do?

Scripture reading: Luke 3:7–14

And the crowds asked him,
"What then should we do?"
Luke 3:10

Advertisements entice buyers with the slogan, "Just do it!" But what is it we're supposed to do? Most of us have a lifetime of experience with the question, "What should I do?" Young adults face choices about career paths, while those a little older often have to wrestle with difficult personal and ethical questions concerning career advancement and "climbing the ladder." Parents weigh decisions about how and where (and in what schools) to nurture their children. Retirees, or those preparing to retire, may wonder whether sharing now will leave them vulnerable later. In the face of changing circumstances – in the realization of responsibility and opportunity – we continually want to know if what we do is enough or right. At each stage of our lives, we ask, "What should I do?"

Who we ask this question of is critical. To ask another "What should I do?" entails trust and vulnerability. In this reading from the gospel of Luke, different groups of people ask John the Baptizer this question, after hearing him give some pretty serious warnings and advice, including the admonition to "bear fruit worthy of repentance." John's answers to the question "What should we do?" are neither easy nor comfortable.

Specifically oriented to each group of questioners, John's first answer encourages everyone listening to live with a spirit of generosity. John's next two responses, directed at tax-collectors and soldiers, encourage honesty and integrity and compassion.

These responses may seem to "state the obvious," yet they remind us that for the world to become a better place, each of us needs to engage in acts of generosity, compassion, and to do everything we do with integrity. No doubt John's responses both challenged and encouraged his listeners, as they do us today.

"What then should I do?" This is a perennial life question, asked in ancient times and today alike. Imagine that you are asking John this question right now. What do you think his answer would be?

Questions for reflection

♦ What insight into your relationship with God and others do you gain from these verses?

♦ What new commitments might you make during this Advent season to engage in acts of generosity and compassion?

Prayer

God of grace, as I search for a deeper relationship with you, I pray that I will be open to the challenge of John's words. I pray that I can open my mind and heart to ways of living with increased generosity, compassion, and integrity. Amen.

∼ December 16 ∼

Trusting in God

Scripture reading: Isaiah 12:2–6

…I will trust, and will not be afraid…
Isaiah 12:2a

In this reading, Isaiah encourages people to rejoice and give thanks for all that God has done and is doing in their midst. They are encouraged to trust and not be afraid, knowing that their trust in God makes it possible to face all circumstances.

There is something about the Season of Advent that causes us to pause and become more aware of God's nearness, of God's presence "in our midst." Hope arises in us out of this awareness, out of a trust that God will always be there for us.

What we know about God is important,
but *what we do with what we know about God is even more important.*
Richard Rohr

What we know about God is that God is about love. If we know that we are beloved by God, then perhaps we can love ourselves and know that we are capable of loving others. What we know about God is that God is trustworthy. If we are able to trust God and not be afraid, then perhaps we will be able to trust ourselves. We will be able to trust that we can face what comes to us on life's journey, without being afraid of those encounters.

Think of a relationship that you trust and value deeply. Ask yourself what words and actions have brought trust and deeper intimacy to that relationship. What did you invest in that relationship? Reflect on how that relationship has changed you.

Now consider these same things as you reflect on your relationship with God: what words and actions have brought deeper trust and intimacy to that relationship; and how are you being changed by your relationship with God?

Questions for reflection

◆   In what ways does the awareness of God's nearness and presence in the midst of your life help to dispel fear?
◆   How do you show trust in God in the way you approach life?

Prayer

Grant me patience, O God, as I wait in hope and trust, waiting for your coming into the world, waiting with the words of an ancient song echoing in my ears:

> *"O come, O Dayspring, come and cheer*
> *Our spirits by thine advent here;*
> *Love stir within the womb of fright,*
> *And death's own shadows put to flight."*
> Amen.

Rejoice

Scripture reading: Philippians 4:4–7

Rejoice in God always; again I will say, Rejoice.
Philippians 4:4

The third Sunday in Advent is often called "Rejoice Sunday," a time when we celebrate the theme of joy. Today, when our world is so filled with stories of misery and oppression, we really need those who believe in joy and who can help to lift the veil of sadness by proclaiming this joy to the world.

Joy is the most infallible sign of the presence of God.
Leon Bloy

In the fourth chapter of the letter to the Philippians, Paul proclaims a message of joy, calling on all believers to live their lives with joy and to trust in the presence of God in their lives. This is also a call for us to recognize joy in our lives – to trust it, believe it, and live it.

Did Paul mean that Christians should always be happy? Not likely. Human nature being what it is, people can't possibly remain in a perpetual state of bliss. But perhaps we can cultivate a deep sense of joy that provides a foundation for the way we live in the world.

Paul goes on to say that Christians should be known for their freedom from anxiety. At first glance this, too, can seem like a nearly impossible piece of advice, like a facile "don't worry…be happy" kind of message that doesn't take into account the real world. In the face of tragedy, grinding sorrow and need, huge inequities and injustice, not to mention the smaller more mundane personal anxieties we carry around with us, how can we possibly not be dragged down with worry and a sense of discouragement?

While there are legitimate reasons for feeling anxiety and despair, the pervasive anxiety that seems so common in daily life is the antithesis of how our faith calls us to live. Instead of being overwhelmed by the concerns we have for ourselves and for others, we can wrap our concerns in prayer, and, with a sense of gratitude for all that God has done and continues to do, hold them up to the light of God's love and care.

Reflect on all of the ways that you experience joy in your life right now. Consider how this joy is a sign of God's presence, and how it can give you the staying power you need to face the vagaries of life.

Questions for reflection

◆ How do your experiences of joy enable you to face times of fear, doubt, and pain?

◆ What do you hear in the word "rejoice" that beckons you to a deeper relationship with God?

Prayer

O God of joy, I pray that your joy will invade my life. I ask for courage to spread joy in the world, as a witness to your presence in my life. Amen.

~ **December 18** ~

God in Our Midst

Scripture reading: Zephaniah 3:14–20

(God) is in your midst…
(God) will renew you in love…
Zephaniah 3:15b, 17b

Gᴏd is in your midst…" All through this reading from Zephaniah, the same message is repeated: God is with you, God has not abandoned you, God is definitely on your side. God is not just the God of your yesterdays. God is the God of your todays and your tomorrows.

Read this passage again noticing all the hopeful words of promise that unfold from the concept of "God in our midst": "Don't be afraid," "God will rejoice over you," "God will remove disaster," "God will bring you home," "God will restore your fortunes." These are the promises of God, powerful words for the people of Zephaniah's time, who lived in fear, under the threat of destruction.

These are also powerful words for us to hear as we struggle with the shadows of fear in our own lives and in the world today, because they remind us that the light of God's promise is unquenchable. Read again each phrase, as if it is being addressed to you. Reflect on the ways in which disaster has been removed during your life journey. Reflect on your experiences of being "brought home" by God. Reflect on the fortunes that God might be restoring in your life right now. Reflect on the ways you have experienced and are experiencing God in your midst.

It is both terrible and comforting to dwell in the
inconceivable nearness of God,
and so to be loved by God that the first and last gift is infinity
and inconceivability itself.
But we have no choice. God is with us.

Karl Rahner

Most of the time in the midst of our busy lives, God seems distant, even unreal. And then, suddenly, for some reason, we become powerfully aware of "God in our midst." It might be during times of fear, or during a moment of transcending beauty. Suddenly we come face to face with a mystery greater than ourselves, and we pause in wonder.

Questions for reflection

- When have you experienced "God in your midst"? In what ways have these experiences been terrible? In what ways have they been comforting?
- In what ways might you open yourself more to the mystery of God's presence and to being renewed in God's love?

Prayer

Loving and eternal God, I long for my life to be renewed in your love. Open the eyes of my soul so that I can always be aware of your presence in the midst of my life. Amen.

～ December 19 ～

Filled with Expectation

Scripture reading: Luke 3:15–18

…the people were filled with expectation…
Luke 3:15a

Do you remember those three groups who asked John, "What should we do?" (Luke 3:10) John's various replies stirred a sense of expectation and speculation in those who listened and watched and waited to see what was going to happen.

Advent, we are told, is about waiting, or learning to wait, in hopeful expectation for the fulfillment of God's promises.

Yet few of us really know *how* to wait, even though we often feel like we are waiting all the time…for the kettle to boil, for the rain to clear, for a situation to improve.

Our experiences of Advent waiting are rarely filled with hopeful expectation. We tend to spend Advent in the same way as we might wait in the queue at the supermarket. Impatiently. Without intention. We distract ourselves with reading the newspaper, or listening to the radio, or grumbling and worrying about everything we have to do to prepare for Christmas.

"And the people were filled with expectation…" But how do we wait for God? Who has taught us this way of being and living?

We seem to have lost the art, if we ever really knew it, of quiet, expectant waiting. Waiting does not come easily. Sometimes, we experience our own powerlessness, because waiting is also a time of letting go, of just being, of not doing.

Waiting patiently in expectation is the foundation of spiritual life.
Simone Weil

Take a few moments to reflect on how you will spend these last few days of Advent. How might you practice the art of waiting in expectation? What you do while you wait depends on what you are waiting for. Consider what you might do as you wait for the breaking in of wonder, the breaking in of eternity.

Questions for reflection

♦   In what ways do you need to relinquish control and allow yourself to wait with patience and expectation?

♦   What renewal and transformation do you seek in your life?

♦   What are some attitudes or actions that you might need to let go of in order to be able to wait expectantly and with wonder?

Prayer

O God, fill me with expectation. Help me create room in my days for waiting in your presence, for opening my whole being to wonder. Amen.

~ **December 20** ~

Sharing Good News

Scripture reading: Luke 3:15–18

So, with many other exhortations,
[John] proclaimed the good news to the people.
Luke 3:18

In this reading, John's conversation with the crowds introduces the one who comes to baptize, not just with water but with spirit and fire. God's reign is coming, embodied in the ministry of Jesus. John announces this good news, and, at the same time, challenges people to reorient their lives in light of it.

"Proclaim the good news…Share the gospel…" These phrases can sometimes make us uncomfortable. We are not sure how we can and should share the good news of God's reign with others. It is good to know that sometimes we do not need to use words. Sometimes the good news of God's love for us and for all people can take shape in our actions, as we reach out to others.

"Sharing as gospel": Once a month, members and friends of a small Presbyterian church in the United States gather on Saturday morning with bags of groceries and sometimes clothing. They prepare a meal, which they then transport to a homeless shelter for individuals and families in a nearby community. They stay to serve the food and visit with the adults and children who have found refuge in that place. They share goods, to be sure. But all who are present share time, words, and presence. They experience "sharing as gospel."

In sharing our anxieties and our love,
our poverty and our prosperity,
we partake of God's divine presence.
Rev. Canaan Banana

Reflect on the ways you have shared your time, your gifts, your caring with others during this Advent season. Your sharing probably happens in a variety of ways, some of which may go unrecognized or unheralded. How does hearing about the sharing actions of others elicit and encourage your own acts of sharing?

Questions for reflection

◆ In what ways have you experienced or participated in "sharing as gospel"?

◆ Where would you like to have or participate in more sharing in your life?

◆ Imagine John standing in those places. If you were to ask, "What should I do?" what do you think John would say?

◆ This may well be the word God is speaking. Now then, what will you do?

Prayer

What then should I do? You call me, O God, to examine my life and to proclaim the good news of your love. Help me to respond to your call to care deeply. Amen.

⁓ **December 21** ⁓

Bread of Tears

Scripture reading: Psalm 80:1–7

You have fed them with the bread of tears....
Psalm 80:5a

Though Advent (which literally means "arrival") has been observed for centuries as a time to contemplate Christ's birth, most people today acknowledge this season with a blank look. For the vast majority of us, the weeks of December have flown by in a flurry of activities, and what should be a time of expectant hope and waiting turns out to be the most stressful time of the year.

It is also a time of conflicting emotions. We can move between eager anticipation and excitement to exhausted apathy. One minute we are excited about getting together with family and friends and the next we feel lonely and overwhelmed. Our hope is mingled with dread, our anticipation with despair. We catch a glimpse of the deeper meaning of the season, yet feel unable to experience it.

The reading from Psalm 80 contains feelings of longing and despair that echo some of the feelings we may experience during the Advent season. There is a sense of absence here, not presence, and of shadow and loneliness. *"You have fed them with the bread of tears...you have made them to drink tears in large measure..."* This verse expresses the kind of grief that can be present in our lives when we have felt lost and despairing.

Reflect on the times in your life when you have "fed on the bread of tears." What does it mean to read these words just before the celebration of Jesus' birth? It means that we acknowledge that there are always difficult times, when we can't celebrate the way we would like to. It means that in the midst of pain and despair, we can reach for God's promise of better things to come. We hold on, at the edge of an event that confirms God's promise and presence in a way that nothing else can or will. We are about to experience the incarnation, "God with us."

For me, the Incarnation is the place, if you will,
where hope contends with fear...
the hope that allows me some measure of peace when
I soldier on in the daily round.

Kathleen Norris

Questions for reflection

◆ What has sustained you during those times when you have "fed on the bread of tears"?

◆ How have you experienced "hope contending with fear" as you move through your daily life?

Prayer

God of grace, help me to feel your comfort and hope when times are difficult. Restore me and dry my tears. Amen.

～ December 22 ～

Blessed Are You

Scripture reading: Luke 1:39–45

And blessed is she who believed that there would be a fulfillment of what was spoken to her by God.
Luke 1:45

In this season of hope, we have read the messages of a number of prophets: Jeremiah, Zechariah, Zephaniah, and John. In today's reading from the gospel of Luke, we hear the voices of two more prophets: Elizabeth, the mother-to-be of John; and Mary, the mother-to-be of Jesus. To the religious faithful in their day, it would have seemed quite unlikely that these two women would be God's prophets, heralds of the Messiah. But in Luke's gospel, this is exactly how God works.

God is full of surprises. God chooses a young peasant woman, Mary, to be the mother of Jesus. God chooses the elderly Elizabeth to bear a son, John. And when these two women meet, surprise is in the air.

Imagine the ordinariness of life that surrounds this holy event. Two pregnant women meet. Elizabeth, feeling the kick of unborn feet, speaks spontaneous and wise words of blessing. Mary, wondering and excited, listens for God in the spoken words of blessing and in the silences. Elizabeth and Mary share a heart-to-heart conversation in a small town in the Judean hills, barely realizing their role in the beginning of a revolution that will transform people's understanding of power and justice.

In the remaining hours before Christmas,
we're the ones who stand on tiptoe eagerly awaiting a new beginning;
we're the ones rummaging through the dress-up box
knowing that transformation is just around the corner.
We want to be part of it.

Ulrike R. M. Guthrie

The prophetic voices of Mary and Elizabeth invite us to be part of the surprising joy and justice of God's reign, bearing this news to the world. Reflect for a few moments on the dreams and visions you carry as you journey through these last few days of Advent. What blessings have you experienced? What blessings have you offered?

Questions for reflection

◆ How does Elizabeth respond to God's activity in her life?
◆ How do you respond to God's activity in your life?
◆ What new beginnings are you waiting for?

Prayer

Surprising God, I find myself in the midst of unexpected and holy times. Like Mary and Elizabeth, may I be filled with joy and hope, open to what you are accomplishing in and through me. Amen.

∼ December 23 ∼

Rebirth of Hope

Scripture reading: Luke 1:46–55

My soul magnifies the Most High,
and my spirit rejoices in God my Saviour…
Luke 1:46–47

In the rest of this reading from the gospel of Luke, we can see how God loves and calls into service all people, including those who may seem meek and ordinary. We are reminded that God's reign of hope and justice comes in ways that surprise us and fill us with joy. In this gospel, peasants bring plenty; women nurture a revolution; and God chooses to work powerfully in and through the very ones who appear powerless.

Mary sings the glory of God's powerful love. She sings because God acts with justice and mercy to lift the lowly; God scatters the proud and feeds the hungry. Mary sings for all the generations who have hoped, and hope even still, for God's promise of justice to be fulfilled in their lives. Even as we wait for the birth of the babe, hope is being born again in today's world through those who work for God's justice. A story from Haiti, the poorest country in the Western Hemisphere, speaks of justice and hope in a place so beset by the ills of the world that one might be tempted to give up hope altogether.

Each day, hundreds of villagers take medications to AIDS victims in the far reaches of Haiti. This AIDS treatment program was started by Dr. Paul Farmer, a Harvard medical professor and anthropologist.

Dr. Farmer has been working in Haiti since he was in his 20s and is committed to bringing life-sustaining medical help to those living with AIDS. One of the biggest obstacles to expanding AIDS treatment in poor countries is the scarcity of doctors, nurses, and high-tech equipment. Dr. Farmer's program, Partners in Health, has minimized reliance on medical professionals by training ordinary citizens in rural Haiti to dispense medicines, draw blood, take X-rays, measure vital signs, and spread the word about how to prevent HIV infection. This program is bringing life and hope to otherwise forgotten people.

Reflect on other stories you have heard or read in which God's justice and hope are being proclaimed and acted out in the world. Though it may seem surprising and, at times, hard to believe, God also chooses to act in our lives. God's Spirit fills us with power so that our ordinary lives might bear God to the world.

Questions for reflection

◆ What do you learn from Mary and Elizabeth about our role in bearing God's love into the world?
◆ What words of hope do you most need in your life? What words of hope do you think the world most needs to hear?
◆ As you prepare to welcome the Christ child into your life again, what reversals might you need to consider in your own life so that you can help bring about God's way of justice in the world?

Prayer

O God, you have created and filled every day with possibility and promise. You have called me to participate in your reign of hope and justice. Help me to be open to what you are accomplishing in and through me. Amen.

Keeping Watch

Scripture reading: Luke 2:1–20

In that region there were shepherds living in the fields,
keeping watch over their flocks by night.
Luke 2:8

A deep mystery surrounds this eve, as we keep watch with shepherds, waiting in hushed and holy anticipation.

Look at the painting on the cover of this book. Immerse yourself in this image: the starry sky, bursting with hope, shimmering in anticipation; the deep peace and comfort in the steady grazing of the seven sheep, surrounded by the dark sentinels of trees, or are they a sacred ring of standing stones?

On Christmas Eve we light candles and ponder the mystery and wonder of this time.

Hush

Sssh.
Can you hear it?
An expectant silence, a hushed anticipation,
as if the very galaxy is holding its breath.

There are some truths even the stars know,
like darkness, like loneliness,
and how the night can be a living thing.

And how once, long ago,
the night waited in wonder
along with the darkness and the loneliness,
for the sound of a baby's cry,

for the miraculous to come down
to the earth mundane.

Lucinda Hynett

Take a few moments to be still. Step outside, if you can, and look up at the sky. Imagine the whole galaxy holding its breath. The time of expectant waiting is almost over…we linger with the shepherds and listen to angels and wait to hear anew the sound of a newborn's cry. And when that cry comes we will know, deep in our souls, that the miraculous has once more come down to earth mundane.

Questions for reflection

♦ What are some of the things you are waiting in wonder for this Christmas Eve?

♦ What good news are you waiting to hear the angels sing?

Prayer

O God, fill me with a sense of awe and wonder. Help me to feel the sacredness of this moment, to sense the hope and holiness that shines through this night. Amen.

∽ December 25 ∽

"God with Us"

Scripture reading: Luke 2:1–20

But the angel said to them, "Do not be afraid…
I am bringing you good news of great joy for all the people:
to you is born this day in the city of David
a Saviour, who is the Messiah…"
Luke 2:10–11

The waiting is over. And all of us who gazed through December windows looking for stars, listening for the sound of angel wings, now see God's promise fulfilled. Our dreaming has given birth to a new reality. Our story tells us that in a manger in Bethlehem, divine mystery is wrapped in earthly swaddling cloths.

Each year, in some awe-filled way, the Christ child is born again into the world. We welcome Emmanuel, God with us, in the vulnerability and tenderness of a baby, bearing hope for the world. On this Christmas Day, heaven touches earth and we will never be the same again. Imagine kneeling on that first Christmas morning, holding the promise of hope in your arms.

"Do not be afraid…" the angels reassure the shepherds, even as they announce the good news. God comes to be with us on lonely dark hillsides, and in the obscure, cobwebbed stable corners of our lives. And this experience of Emmanuel, God with us, invites us to transform our places of fear and self-centeredness into actions of love and openness

and solidarity. Imagine standing with shepherds in the starlit darkness, hearing the message, *"to you is born…"*

"And suddenly there was with the angel a multitude of the heavenly host…" Imagine dancing among the stars with the angels, full of hope and radiant joy.

Emmanuel: God with us.
God in the world.
God in our homes.
Emmanuel: God with us.
God born in our souls.
Emmanuel: God with us.
God beside us. God within us.

Questions for reflection

◆ What is the good news announced by the angels for you this year?
◆ In what ways have you experienced awe and glory and a sense of "God with us" in your Christmas celebrations?

Prayer

Incarnate God, thank you for your love that shines through the Christmas story. Help me to know and feel and celebrate your presence this day. Amen.

~ **December 26** ~

Incarnation

Scripture reading: Luke 2:1–20

*But Mary treasured these things,
pondering them in her heart.*
Luke 2:19

O ur Christmas story tells us that the shepherds heeded the voice of the angel and went to Bethlehem to "see this thing that has taken place." There they do indeed find a newborn baby and they announce the identity of this babe in echoes of the words spoken by the angel. And all who listen are amazed. When have we let ourselves be amazed again by this familiar story?

The one proclaimed as Saviour and Messiah begins life, so our story goes, in a stable, attended by animals and heralded by shepherds. No wonder Mary pondered these words in her heart. Imagine what is going through her mind as she holds that newborn, as she rests, exhausted from labor. What emotions gripped her as she thought about the birthing? What did she think, pray, feel, remember? From where did she draw her strength? Did she feel the blessing in this holy birth?

*What good is it to me
if this eternal birth of the divine Son
takes place unceasingly
but does not take place within myself?*

What good is it to me
for the Creator to give birth to [his/her] Son
if I do not also give birth to him
in my time and my culture?

Meister Eckhart

From this side of the story, we look through the lens of Christian tradition, which speaks of the Incarnation, of the divine God becoming a human baby. Here we touch a mystery that transcends human understanding. It is the mystery of divinity shining through a human being named Jesus. And we are called to participate in this mystery.

Questions for reflection

◆ What do the stories of Jesus' birth tell you about God? About human beings?

◆ In what ways are you giving birth to Jesus in your own time and culture?

Prayer

Creator God, thank you for the mystery of incarnation. Open my heart to the wonder and mystery of this birth. Help me to hear again the song of the angels and to participate in a new birthing. Amen.

~ December 27 ~

Someone Unexpected

Scripture reading: Micah 5:2–5a

But you, O Bethlehem…one of the little clans…
from you shall come forth one who is to rule…
and he shall be the one of peace.

Micah 5:5

One of the major themes of the Bible is that God acts in unexpected ways. This reading from the prophet Micah speaks of great and glorious things coming from an unexpected place. Speaking during a turbulent period in Israel's history, Micah declares that a new ruler will shepherd God's people in the ways of peace. Surprisingly, we learn that this ruler will be born in the small town of Bethlehem. While Bethlehem was the family home of King David, this announcement contradicted the expectation that God's Messiah would come from Jerusalem, the royal city.

The Messiah, the one "whose origin is from of old, from ancient days," will be born in an ordinary, homely little town. God doesn't come in vast, showy ways – God comes to the ordinary place and to the ordinary person.

Not only is the *place* of incarnation unexpected and unlikely, but the "one who comes" is described in unexpected ways. The one who comes is not a champion or a diplomat or a king; the one who comes will be a shepherd – one who stands with, one who feeds, one who offers security, one who is a sign of peace.

The message for us is that just like God can bring forth a Messiah from ordinary, little Bethlehem, God can act in surprising, unexpected ways in our own lives. Most of us have experienced God's grace in surprising ways, perhaps through the lives of individuals who seem to be unlikely candidates for such ministry. Sometimes we wonder if our *own* lives have touched others with God's love and presence. Occasionally, we hear that we've made a difference. Often we don't know. Our challenge is to rejoice in our participation in God's reign and to keep on trying.

> *When a place or time seems touched by God, it is an overshadowing, a sudden eclipsing of my priorities and plans. But even in terrible circumstances and calamities, in matters of life and death, if I sense that I am in the shadow of God, I find light, so much light that my vision improves dramatically. I know that holiness is near.*

Kathleen Norris, *Amazing Grace*

Questions for reflection

◆ When have you experienced God's holiness in unexpected, surprising ways?

◆ In what unexpected ways has God acted and spoken into your life and into the life of our world?

Prayer

O God of the unexpected, bless me with surprises. Bless me with your spirit and open me to experiences of the holy in this coming year. Amen.

Dreaming the Future

Scripture reading: Isaiah 52:7–10

Your sentinels lift up their voices, together they sing for joy;
for in plain sight they see the return of the Lord to Zion.
Isaiah 52:8

W hen the people of Israel were in exile in Babylon, the prophet Isaiah committed his energies to nourishing hope among them. The prophet encouraged them to dream the future into the present. This poem expresses what this might look like in our own lives.

Praying through the Thick of It
You must give in to the seduction
of silence. Listen for things central:
the sound of air moving in and out
of your being, the soft bump of blood

drumming at your core, the small
noises deep in the ears when different
parts of your body call attention
to themselves. Then listen past them.

Squint your hearing as you might your
eyes and seek some sense of music
in the air around you. If you come back
empty-handed you're on your way.

The mind will play hide and seek with
everything you know. Let each game
pass like summer storms on a windy day.
Follow after none of them. Stay put.

That's more than half the matter. Dig
into the celestial machinery with your heels,
stand your ground, become everything
the universe needs to know about itself.

Let what you are speak to what always is.
Let yourself be like a leaf sailing on the river
God, a bit of matter and light being swept
out to the enormous sacredness of the sea.

Let yourself dissolve into it like salt,
like snow, like sugar in hot tea. Become
what it is, for what it is is who you are,
a visible manifestation of an invisible thing.

Fredrick Zydek

Questions for reflection

♦ What dream do you think God is dreaming for the future this Christmas?

♦ In what ways are you prepared to invest your time and energy and prayer into aligning yourself with God's dream, helping to dream this future into the present?

Prayer

Eternal God, fill me with your vision and perception. Help me dream into reality a future that is world-changing and life-changing. Amen.

◯ **December 29** ◯

Visioning God's Reign

Scripture reading: Isaiah 52:7–10

How beautiful upon the mountains
are the feet of the messenger who announces peace…
For God has comforted the people,
God has redeemed Jerusalem.
Isaiah 52:7, 9

Your God reigns," says the messenger in Isaiah…the kingdom of justice and of righteousness that we have been waiting for has finally arrived. But has it really? The exiles who listened to these words probably didn't think so. They had no real evidence that God was anywhere nearby. Nothing in their situation suggested that God had finally returned and that the future was now better and that peace would reign once again.

"Glory to God in the highest heaven, and on earth peace…" sing the angels in first-century Palestine, to people who had no evidence that peace would reign once again. And today, in the 21st century, do we have much evidence of God's peace either?

But the prophet, and the angels, and other messengers invite us to dream that these things are already so. We are not offered a quick fix. Instead, we are asked to see the future not as something we create by our own doing, but as something that comes toward us, open with unlimited possibilities.

What is it that you dream for yourself, for your family, for your community, for the world? As this year draws to a close, what kind of future do you envision? What you envision already happening can inspire and motivate you to work for the fulfillment of that dream.

> *Unless you live as if the world you imagine exists,*
> *the world you imagine will never exist.*
> **Alice Walker**

Christmas is not the end of the story. The birth of Christ reminds us that God is dreaming a future and inviting us to participate in it. Reflect on how you might do this.

Questions for reflection

◆ In what ways can you be one who "announces peace" and "brings good news" in your daily life?

◆ What dream do you think God is dreaming for the future?

◆ How might you participate in this dream?

◆ Does your way of life communicate your belief that God's reign of peace and justice is possible?

Prayer

O God, you invite me to take part in your dreaming of the future. Help me to participate with an open, expectant heart, to proclaim the possibility of peace on earth and goodwill to all. Amen.

⌒ December 30 ⌒

Praise God!

Scripture reading: Psalm 148

*Praise God all angels…praise God sun and moon;
praise God all you shining stars…and highest heavens.*

Psalm 148:2–3

Psalm 148 is a good psalm to read during the Christmas season because it celebrates the profligate generosity of God. The whole of creation praises God the creator, celebrating the giver of life. God speaks, and the created world bears witness to God's grace. God speaks, and the Word becomes flesh, and in that Word is holiness.

Think about one of your favorite places in nature. Imagine yourself going there, walking through this place, feeling your thoughts become quiet as you look for signs of God's glory in this space. What part of Creation is praising God here? In what way does this feel like a place where "God lives"?

Besides celebrating God as the author of creation, the words of Psalm 148 also celebrate our relationship with God. As the calendar year draws to a close, pause to reflect on how you've grown in your relationship with God over the past year. Reflect on the following statements, writing down words and phrases that occur to you as you think about each of the following things:

- something you heard or saw that filled you with awe for God's creation;

- a time when you sensed God with you in a deep way; a time when you wondered about God's activity in your life;
- a person who spoke of and/or demonstrated God's love for you.

Use some of the words and phrases that you have noted to write your own psalm of praise for God's care in your life, and for your hope in God's presence in the year to come.

Consider the spiritual practice of "praying the psalms" as a discipline for the coming year. The psalms can remind us to be reverent, to strive for a godly life, and to practice justice and righteousness. They can lift us from the "dailyness" of life and help us focus on God. As long as we are praying the psalms, we are connected to something beyond our own experience.

One way to pray a psalm is to choose a word or phrase to carry with you for the day. You might choose from Psalm 148, "God's glory is above the earth and heaven." Make this your prayer for the day. Be especially attentive to the word "glory." Where do you see signs of God's glory? How is what you say and do reflecting God's glory?

Questions for reflection

- What images in Psalm 148 help you to express your feelings about Christmas?
- In what ways can the psalms inform and guide your spiritual journey?

Prayer

Holy, holy, holy are you, O God. Your joy gives me life. Your love and faithfulness sustain me. Holy, holy, holy are you, O God. Amen.

∼ **December 31** ∼

God's Glory

Scripture reading: Psalm 148

Let them praise the name of God, for God's name is exalted;
God's glory is above earth and heaven.

Psalm 148:13

R ead this psalm again, through the lens of this paraphrase, written as a salute to the new year, as the days are beginning to grow longer in the Northern Hemisphere:

> *Come and join the joyful dance of life!*
> *Celebrate each moment of increasing light!*
> *When the sun comes out after the snow,*
> *when the south wind blows the blizzards away,*
> *all of creation creeps out of its caves*
> *to soak up the welcome warmth...*
>
> *The planet throbs with the pulse of life;*
> *heartbeats pound their passionate rhythm.*
> *Princes and popes, outlaws and outcasts,*
> *all races, all colors, all ages, all species,*
> *swirl like galaxies glowing in a summer night.*
> *The Lord God made them all.*

There are no wallflowers in God's great dance;
each piece of creation has its own part to play.
We humans live and die;
our communities come and go,
our empires rise and fall;
The Lord God made them all…
And the dance goes on.

James Taylor, *Everyday Psalms*

The words of this psalm paint a magnificent portrait of God: majestic, creative, authoritative, compassionate, dependable, glorious. Spend a few moments reflecting on each of these characteristics. Through the poetry of the psalms, we begin to comprehend the dynamic mystery of God. Though the psalms are addressed to God, they are not for God alone. They help us to name our own experiences of the holy.

Questions for reflection

- How do these characteristics match your image of God?
- What image of God might you carry with you into the new year?
- All creation is called to praise God. In what ways is your life an act of praise?

Prayer

Creator God, in this season of radiance, I give thanks for your faithfulness, your compassion, and the mystery of your holy love. Amen.

~ **January 1** ~

In the Beginning

Scripture reading: John 1:1–14

In the beginning was the Word...
John 1:1

The gospel of John does not give us a birth story about Jesus, as do the gospels of Matthew and Luke. Instead, the author begins with a poem or a hymn about Jesus, and links his arrival to the beginning of time. The writer of John's gospel uses Word to speak of Christ, and of the mysterious, creative force of God, speaking things into existence.

The Word was first,
the Word present to God,
God present to the Word.
The Word was God,
in readiness for God from day one.
Eugene H. Peterson, *The Message*

"In the beginning..." This birth story is like the story of creation, but this time God does more than say words over creation. God places the Word *in* creation, like yeast in a loaf of bread. Jesus came as God's Word, entering time and space to become human. Jesus changed the world by living out the words "grace, truth, and light." He chose to use words to bring life, not hurt; and we can too.

Read the whole passage, John 1:1–14, making note of the words and images that stand out for you. Words have great power to heal, to make change, to bring hope. How can your words make a difference? How might your words bring healing, liberty, or comfort?

The Word of God is always "in the beginning."
And this means
that it is always in the process of being born
and is always already born.

Meister Eckhart

During the coming weeks look at what is happening in the world around you, and ask yourself the question, "How is the Word of God speaking here?"

Questions for reflection

◆ On this first day of a new year, what words will guide you through the coming year?

◆ What does it mean to always be ready to welcome the Christ child into your heart and mind and body?

Prayer

O God, you are the continual maker.
Every day you make the world.
Every day you make meaning and purpose.
Every day you make grace and wonder and joy.
Help me be aware of where your Word is speaking into my life.
Amen.

⌒ January 2 ⌒

Born of God

Scripture reading: John 1:1–14

And the Word became flesh and lived among us…full of grace and truth.
John 1:14

The Greek word (John was writing in Greek) for "word" is *logos,* which is another form of the word "logic." Jesus (*Logos* made flesh) helps to "make sense" of God and of how the world can be. Jesus in human form makes God no longer seem out of reach or incomprehensible. God is touchable and real. The gospels portray Jesus as someone who spent time with his friends. He argued. He ate and drank. He slept and worried. He cried. This is what God's word and wisdom does in human form. It lives in the muddiest bits of the world.

"The word became flesh and blood and moved into the neighborhood…" We all have times of thinking that nobody will ever understand us, that there are no words to express our grief, our delight, our joy, our pain. And it's true – often there are no words. God sent a human being to embody the words, to make them come to life.

John tells us that Jesus came to "make sense" of God's message to the world, but John tells us this in language that is laden with mystery, meaning, and metaphor.

What came into existence was Life,
And the Life was Light to live by.
The Life-Light blazed out of the darkness;
The darkness couldn't put it out.

Eugene H. Peterson, *The Message*

Life-light...Now we're hearing that with the coming of the Word in flesh and blood, there is a new light for our world, a light that points us back to God. Imagine a cartoon where the characters have a light bulb suddenly turn on above their heads and we know that they've suddenly "got it." John is telling us that Jesus is like that light bulb for us. If we look at the way Jesus lived, then we'll see what God is like, and we'll see the way that God wants us to live.

Questions for reflection

◆ What is it like to think of God as being this human?

◆ What situations in your life or community would benefit from a new light shining on them?

◆ How does God's word and wisdom, embodied in Jesus, help you to make sense of your life?

◆ How might you use your words to bring light and life to the world?

Prayer

O God, help me to have times of silence so that I can hear your Word whispering into my world. Help me to know how to put your Word into actions in this world. Amen.

~ **January 3** ~

Holy and Beloved

Scripture reading: Colossians 3:12–17

*Clothe yourselves with compassion,
kindness, humility, meekness, and patience.*
Colossians 3:12

This reading from Paul's letter to the Colossians is like a word portrait of what a Christian community is called to be. It speaks of offering our inner and outer lives, our thoughts, and our actions to God.

"Holy and beloved…" Paul begins by identifying the Colossians as holy and beloved. The degree to which we can see each other as holy is a measure of the degree to which we can express our love for each other. An old story tells of an abbot whose monastery was not doing very well. The monks were constantly bickering and complaining. The abbot had a friend in a nearby town, an old rabbi. He shared his discouragement with his friend and the rabbi offered this advice: "Always remember that one of you may be the Messiah." This didn't make a lot of sense to the abbot, but he returned to the monastery and shared the message with the monks. As time went by, the attitudes and behaviors of the monks began to change, as each one treated the other as if that one might be the Messiah. Soon relationships were transformed and nothing was ever the same in that monastery.

To show great love for God and our neighbour
we need not do great things.
It is how much love we put in the doing that makes
our offering something beautiful for God.

Mother Teresa

"Compassion, kindness…" Look at all the characteristics named as the foundation of living in community. These are important ingredients in any relationship. Without these qualities, life in community might be almost impossible. Reflect on how these qualities are lived out in your relationships with family, friends, and work colleagues.

Questions for reflection

◆ What do you think of Paul's practical advice on how to "feel at home" in one's relationship with God and the community of faith?

◆ Where do you need compassion and kindness and patience in your life? Who must you be ready to forgive?

◆ Think about those people with whom you have difficult relationships. How might thinking of these ones as if they were the Messiah transform your relationships?

Prayer

O God, I ask that love be born in me as purpose, strength, courage, and hope. Amen.

~ **January 4** ~

Words of Wisdom

Scripture reading: Luke 2:41–52

And all who heard him were amazed at his understanding and his answers.
Luke 2:47

The gospel of Luke is the only gospel that includes this story about Jesus. As a 12-year-old, Jesus had probably already gone through the ceremony of *bar mitzvah* (becoming a "son of the law") and therefore was now required to accompany his parents to the seven-day festival of Passover in Jerusalem. There Jesus can't resist the chance to learn more about God from the teachers who gathered in the temple to discuss and debate aspects of the faith. Spend a few moments imagining what Jesus and the religious leaders might have talked about together.

Consider what it means to live firmly grounded in God's word and in the traditions of the faith community. At all ages, our lives are grounded in God's love and nurtured through the collective wisdom of God's people. What does it mean to carry this wisdom into daily living? Where do you look for guidance for faithful living in God's world? There are a variety of opinions about what constitutes wisdom. Discerning God's wisdom and ordering our lives according to God's way is a lifelong process.

Think about "words of wisdom" you have received from older people in your life. Read the following statements about wisdom, reflecting for a few moments on each one.

To conquer fear is the beginning of wisdom.
Bertrand Russell

If you have knowledge, let others light their candles in it.
Margaret Fuller

The road of excess leads to the palace of wisdom.
William Blake

Great wisdom may resemble foolishness.
Chinese proverb

The invariable mark of wisdom is to see the miraculous in the common.
Ralph Waldo Emerson

As a solid rock is not shaken by the wind, wise people falter not amidst blame and praise.
Dhammapada 6:81 (Buddhist scripture)

[Wisdom] leads me to ever stronger growth and draws me more fully toward inner freedom.
Joyce Rupp

Question for reflection

◆ What "words of wisdom" do you want to carry with you into the coming year?

Prayer

Wise and knowing God, may I be open to the wisdom of the ages coming in unexpected places. May I continue to grow in wisdom, faith, and understanding. Amen.

～ January 5 ～

Growing in Wisdom

Scripture reading: Luke 2:41–52

And Jesus increased in wisdom and in years,
and in divine and human favor.
Luke 2:52

From what we have experienced in our own lives we can guess that the youth who returned to Nazareth was not the same person who had left to travel up to Jerusalem. Jesus had now claimed a relationship with God, which was proclaimed in the stories of his birth. His horizons had been widened. His mind was probably brimming with new ideas. He had been caught up in ideas and insights that would echo in his mind in the months to come.

Think about when this has happened in your own life. An experience happens that leaves a deep impression. A life-shift happens and we are never again the same. Insight is gained, new wisdom received.

We collect much wisdom over the years, cherishing some and discarding some. Nearly all of us have experienced how some of what we once considered to be wisdom has changed over the course of our lifetime.

The gospel story ends with the words, *"And Jesus increased in wisdom and years..."* telling us that Jesus continued to learn and grow in wisdom and understanding. Through growth and maturity, wisdom is honed.

There are seven traits of the wise:
> *They do not speak in the presence of those wiser than themselves;*
> *They do not interrupt when a colleague speaks;*
> *They do not rush out with a rejoinder;*
> *They ask questions that are relevant,*
> *   and give answers that are logical;*
> *They deal with first things first and last things last;*
> *They readily admit when they do not know about a matter;*
> *They acknowledge the truth.*

Rabbi Jose ben Kisma, Talmud (Mishnah, Aboth)

Today's story illustrates the importance of continuing to explore and learn as we move through life. You might like to make a list of some "New Year's resolutions" to foster your growth in wisdom, faith, and understanding.

Questions for reflection

- In what ways are you continuing to grow in wisdom, faith, and understanding?
- What might you want to begin doing this year in order to nurture the growth of wisdom in your spiritual journey?

Prayer

Go with the Spirit, letting God guide you as you grow. Let what you are speak to what always is. Know that God, the source of true wisdom, is in every place, holding you as you grow in wisdom, faith, and understanding.

~ **January 6** ~

Follow the Star!

Scripture reading: Matthew 2:1–12

They set out; and there, ahead of them,
went the star that they had seen at its rising,
until it stopped over the place where the child was.
When they saw that the star had stopped, they were overwhelmed with joy.

Matthew 2:9b–10

Think for a moment about these stargazers, these wise ones from distant places who were so sure that their destiny and the destiny of the world were written in the stars. In what ways do we long to be like them, to have a star to follow as we journey into this new year?

"Star of wonder, star of light, star of royal beauty bright…" These seekers saw wisdom in the stars and followed the star trail to find the new light that had come into the world. There is radiance in the world, hidden from many, but visible to those who know where to look, to those who have their eyes open wide.

This part of our Christmas story is a curious mixture of science and mystery. Auspicious stars, guided travel through the wilderness…all leading to an encounter with God. This is what Epiphany is about… revelation, insight, mystery, and the offering of gifts; opening up our hearts and hands to give gold, and frankincense, and myrrh. When have you wanted to be like those seekers, embarking on one grand adventure?

But the story is also about power-hungry kings, and secret meetings, and signs in dreams, and violence. There are choices to be made and the journey isn't always straightforward. Think about the times when it was hard for you to see where the star was leading. Think about times when your quest was affected by someone's paranoia.

The story of Epiphany tells us that there is light and glory in the world, sometimes hidden, but shining through for those who can see it, a radiance that can't be overcome by cunning or violence. We are invited again and again to follow the star and to become spiritual adventurers in search of a more full and authentic life. We are invited to a lifetime of insights, epiphanies, and revelations on our pilgrim journey.

> *You are the deep innerness of all things,*
> *the last word that can never be spoken.*
> *To each of us you reveal yourself differently:*
> *to the ship as a coastline, to the shore as a ship.*
> **Rainer Maria Rilke**

Questions for reflection

◆ What are your guiding stars on your spiritual journey?
◆ How is God being revealed to you as you move out into this new year?

Prayer

God of stars and epiphanies, guide me in light and in darkness to follow your leading and to recognize your presence. Create in me an unending Epiphany. Amen.

WoodLake

imprint of Wood Lake Publishing Inc

Named for the original company, the WoodLake imprint
continues the long tradition of publishing profoundly usable
books and program resources. From the beginning, WoodLake
projects have been inclusive, truth-seeking, religious, life-
affirming, and have dealt positively with life and faith. While the
spiritual journey often begins on the inside with an individual,
WoodLake titles also challenge readers to move outward,
to express faith in ways that support the earth and all her
creatures.

From David Sparks' series *Prayers to Share A,B, and C,* to sermon
and worship resources such as *Creative Worship,* to youth group
and children's resources from *The Whole People of God Library*
series, to children's stories, music collections, Vacation Bible
School modules, and books on the present and future of the
church – WoodLake has been providing stimulating reading and
eminently practical group resources for 25 years.

WoodLake is a trusted Canadian name for people in mainline
faith communities

Resources for people of faith

Seasonal Resources
Advent, Christmas, and Epiphany

The Midwife's Story
Meditations for Advent Times
Nancy Reeves
Woodcuts by Margaret Kyle
An invitation to use the Advent season as a time to prepare to
become a more intentional revealer of God's will.
$18.00

Simplify and Celebrate
Embracing the Soul of Christmas
Alternatives
Reclaiming the joy and peace of the Christmas season.
$19.95

Treasury of Celebrations
*Create Celebrations that Reflect Your Values and
Don't Cost the Earth*
Alternatives
This big book of plans, tips, and stories channels the desire to
celebrate towards activities that truly nourish the human spirit.
$24.95

The Birth and Childhood Stories of Jesus
The Family Story Bible Curriculum Module 1
Peggy Evans
Complete Storytelling kit with video and 32-page planning guide
helps you share these stories with children aged 3-10.

$64.95

OR ORDER FROM WOOD LAKE PUBLISHING INC

essential spiritualty for our day

PHONE: 1.800.663.2775 or FAX: 1.888.841.9991 or www.woodlakebooks.com

Seasonal Resources
Lent

Easter Stories
The Family Story Bible Curriculum Module 2
Julie Elliott
Based on The Family Story Bible this complete storytelling kit helps you share these wonderful and difficult stories with children aged 3-10.
$64.95

General

Living the Christ Life
Rediscovering the Seasons of the Christian Year
Louise Mangan and Nancy Wyse with Lori Farr
This valuable program resource for clergy, worship planners, and lay leaders offers practical tools for celebrating the Christian Year at church and at home.
$34.95

Creative Worship
Service from Advent to Pentecost
Ian Price and Carolyn Kitto
Poems, readings, songs and other ideas to build creative worship services covering the major seasons of the Christian year.
$24.95

Creative Worship 2
Services for Special Days
Compiled by Ian Price
This compilation comes from a call to churches across Canada, the USA, and Australia, to submit liturgies and orders of worship.
$29.95